"Can y'all tell me how to remove aphids from my privates?"

THE GARDEN CLERK'S DICTIONARY

TRUE STORIES FROM
REAL GARDEN CLERKS
AND GARDENERS IN AMERICA
AND THE REST OF THE WORLD

From The Library Of
Cheri Charleville

edited & illustrated
by Dan Heims

First published in 2005 by
Dan Heims in Portland, OR, USA

Ordering single copies or
discounted multiple copies (12) can be fulfilled by:
Dan Heims, 6663 SW Bvtn Hills Hwy #223, Portland, OR 97225

Additional anecdotes, name corruptions, funny
hort. pictures and garden silliness can be sent to:
Dan Heims, 6663 SW Bvtn Hills Hwy #223, Portland, OR 97225
or *hortiholic@comcast.net*

Editor: Dan Heims
Illustrator: Dan Heims

Proofreaders: Lynne Bartenstein & Susan Narizny
Cover Model: Justine Metteer

Thanks to Keith Kirsten for excerpts from *"Blooming Quotes,"* 2002
www.keithkirsten.com/books3.htm

APOLLO
GRAPHICS
INCORPORATED

Printed by Apollo Graphics
5104 NE Oregon Street
Portland, OR 97213
503.288.9191 tel.

ISBN # 0-9765206-0-5

THANKS TO: Greenland Garden Centre, Pam Whiteley/Mary Smith Associates, Amy McDowell, Thurman Maness, Rita Spray, Fred Spicer, Barbara from SC, Nancy Medveck, Rick Ray, Mark Johnson, Mike Sikes, Dave Creech, John Wachter, Susan Ludwig, Beth Taylor (Bjelkes), Pam Beck, Gerard Amerongen, Helen Schaal, T. Schrum, Angela Treadwell Palmer, Chuck Pavlich, Ellen Deely, Tom Karasek, Kathy Koral, Kathy Freeland, Margaret Lauterbach, Todd Davis, Wilma Penland, Gary Vanburen, Baldassare Mineo, John Valleau, Mary Wilson, Dan Hinkley, Matt Gardiner, Joyce K. Williams, Ann Hoffman, Cindy Gilberg, Kirsten Ego, Noelle, Connie Christians, Tina Dixon, Ted Stephens, Joe Martin, Heather Pratt, Jim Marshall, Roger Wimpfheimer, Vinnie Drzewucki, Bob Weslyn, Greg Speichert, Tony Avent, Sean Hogan, Becky Stewart, Bob Stewart, Terry Wibberg, Sinclair Adam, Stephanie Cohen, Lynn Cohen, Linda, Christa, Becky Dean, Margaret, Jerry, Stephanie, Harry the Rosemeister, Jan, Pam Youngsman, Charolett, Alan Bush, Sam Jones, Ken Brown, Carol, Debbie, Gary, Rebecca Chesin, Janet Egger, Dawn Hummel, Pam Bennett, Laura Morning, Donna, Michelle Charriere, Dan Bissonnette, Ralph Siferd, Lynne Bartenstein, and too many others to mention.

To my professor, Dr. McCallister Ruff
Who opened my eyes to the botanical wonders of the
world with charm, grace, and most of all, humor

For more fun, go to these web sites!

Shady Deals Nursery:
   http://members.tripod.com/~Hatch_L/shady.html/

Garden Humour from England:
   http://home.golden.net/~dhobson/

Terra Nova's site: www.terranovanurseries.com

More: http://www.geocities.com/homegardener/humor.htm

FOREWORD

After five years of cajoling garden clerks, TV and radio hosts, help desk clerks, nursery owners, and friends, I have pulled together a book to unveil the mystery of the customer. Gathering information at every plant show and convention and every garden shop and nursery I entered, I found a common bond of comical exasperation. Some wonderful tidbits came from tattered collections kept by the cash register, and my favorite poem was a piece from the 1930s found on a wall in a back room of a Kentucky nursery. So, here's to all the wonderful people who helped this book become a reality. I remain,

Horticulturally yours,

TABLE OF CONTENTS

THE INFORMATION DESK

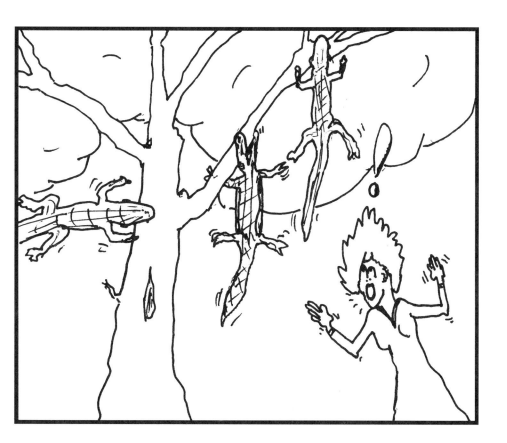

One day a customer came in and asked what she can do about alligators in her trees. I was rather amazed and startled by this and the visual it gave me. I also knew that there are no known alligators to be found roaming suburban gardens here in Westbury, New York. Further questioning revealed she meant to say "caterpillars" were in her trees.

A slightly cynical clerk was asked how you tell a male holly from a female. "Oh, just look under the leaves..."

Two very common questions asked of information desks were "Do I take the plant out of the pot before I plant it?" and "Do I have to water it?"

Customer: "I'd like that shrub that flowers in early spring and has no leaves . . ."

I work at Gerardi's Nursery and Garden Center in O'Fallon, IL. I had a customer ask me for "one of those Uncle Wiggley bushes." What he actually wanted was a *Weigela*.

Allergic couple: "Do you have any sporeless ferns?"
Clerk: "Why do you need sporeless ferns?"
Allergic couple: "We're both terribly allergic to spores."
Clerk: "So why do you need sporeless ferns?"
Allergic couple: "We're driven to have them!"

One of our most hilarious questions was from a telephone call, in which a lady asked, "You keep advertising these paperwhite bulbs. Since when did garden centers start carrying light bulbs, are they special for growing plants???" As well, numerous times we have been asked for Miracle Whip™, instead of Miracle Grow™.

I'll never forget when working at Bennett's Greenhouses in Indiana, all these ladies coming in asking for ponies and pennies; it was May before I realized they wanted peonies.

One customer came into our nursery and asked, "Which bushes can we buy for the front yard and which for the back yard?" Playing his game [our nursery was evenly divided by a road], I said, "left side, front, right side, back," and he was very careful to keep two carts separate... I'm still laughing about that one!

Customer in late September, Zone 6b:
"I understand you specialize in rare plants."
"That's right. . ."
"Do you have any dill?"

I work at Suburban Lawn and Garden in Overland Park, KS. The following is a customer's query about a floating water plant she had just purchased: "Now, if its leaves curl up, does that mean it's too dry?"

Customer: "What plants grow in full sun?"

Customer: "Have you got any of those annuals that come up every year?"
Clerk: "Yes, in the Perennial section."

Customer: "Does Roundup™ kill good plants too?"

When I was manning the Extension service telephone for Master Gardener certification years ago, a woman called and demanded to know what side of her house she should put her garden on. I asked "Which side is the sunniest?"
"I don't know. The sun isn't up when I leave for work, and it has set before I arrive home," she replied. She again demanded to know which side to put her garden on, so I finally said "the south side," after she said she thought the house faced north. No idea how she planned on tending a garden.

Customer: "Why is my azalea dying? Its flowers are dropping off!"
Clerk: "How long have you had it?"
Customer: "About 3 weeks."
Clerk: "Then it's done blooming."
Customer: "What! I thought they bloomed all summer!"

In summer: "I planted those shrubs you sold me, and they are all turning brown. I watered them really good when I planted them . . . should I water them again?"

Customer: "My topiary graft died on top. Can I drill a hole and put a new one in?"

Asked of Dave Creech: "If I plant one of these Norway maples today, when would I have to cut it down?"

Question to Bob Stewart: "When is the last spring frost in our area?"
Bob: "For your area, April 25th is listed as the last frost date."
"What time on April 25th?"

Question to Bob: "What should I do about holes in my cabbage plants?"
Bob answers: "This is caused by the cabbage looper; spray with B.T. [Bacillus thuringensis]"
A week later, the same person calls back.
"I sprayed with B.T. but the holes didn't close up; what did I do wrong?"

We received a call at the local Master Gardener office from a lady with a Japanese beetle problem.
"How can I encourage the *good* Japanese beetles and kill the bad ones"?
The Master Gardener replied that there are no "good" Japanese beetles, only bad ones..
"Yes, there are!", the caller argued. "The ones on top that are trying to eat the ones chewing on the plants!"
This became a time for tact to tell the caller what they were really doing!

Customer [calling from her vacation home]: How often do I have to water them? I'm only up here for a week and nothing will grow there–not even grass… What kind of tree would you recommend? [plastic?–Dan]

Customer: "Do peppers grow above or below ground?"

Customer: "It's got a flower that looks like a little hat" [petunia– Dan]

Customer: Do you have "that green shrubbery" or "that plant"… It's got green leaves…You know! . . ."

On a radio gardening talk show, a caller who heard that it was a good time to put lime on his lawn wanted to know how many to buy and how do you squeeze them.

A nother talk show host was asked:
"Where can I get poison ivy seeds?"
"Whatever for?" responded the host.
"To stop the damn kids from crossing through my property."
"Do you really think that that would stop them?"
"Listen honey, everyone understands the international language of
 itch…"

"Do you sell Oregon natives?"
"Yes, we do!"
"Then would you have any Himalayan honeysuckle?"

Customer calling clerk: "Is this a good time to move my hostages?"
[hostas – Dan]

7

ANIMAL PROBLEMS

At an Olympia, WA, garden center, an elderly gentleman (slightly hard of hearing) came in with some notched rhody leaves and wanted to know what was chewing them.
Chuck Pavlich responded, "Looks like root-weevils."
The gent replied, "Root Weasels?!! Oh my, how do you kill *them*?"

After giving up on all the chemical and natural sprays to repel deer, the exasperated party asked the southern radio host what the best thing was to keep deer away.
He replied, "Lead." After a pregnant pause, the host conveyed that an explosive charge was necessary to dispel the lead. The caller finally understood that a gun was being suggested...

While giving a talk in Arkansas, Dan Heims polled the group on deer-repellents. One of the group members said "I use tiger fur; it works amazingly well."
Dan's reply was, "Yeah, but wasn't it a bitch to get?"

"How do I apply the deer repellent on the deer?"

9

I
WANT
MY
MONEY
BACK!

A customer called B&D Lilies for credit because none of his Asiatic lilies grew. The result of the ensuing inquisition was that he thought they were water lilies and had planted them underwater!

Customer: "These seed potatoes didn't produce! Plants got big; no spuds."
Clerk: "Did you dig them?"
Customer: "Dig them?"

"I ordered a flat of hellebores from you, and when I opened the box today, they were dead. I want my money back."
When did you receive them?
"About six weeks ago."

Back in the late seventies I worked for a department store, managing the garden center. I was on lunch and got called to the department to handle a problem. When I got there, a woman is obviously very upset. It went something like this:

"May I help you?"

"Yes, I want my money back."

"What seems to be wrong?"

"You are selling bad manure!"

"Bad manure?"

"Yes this is composted cattle manure and every time I use it, it burns my plants! I only use composted COW manure and it never burns!"

"Give the lady her money back."

How could you argue with that kind of logic? She remained a loyal customer for years. And yes, she only ever bought cow manure.

Another story was the day a customer came in with aphids on his tomato plants. Upon being shown the right product to use to control them, he then demanded we give the product to him for free, claiming that no one told him his tomato plants might get bugs.

People are always bringing in a dead plant to our independent nursery and saying, "I bought these at (enter box-store name) and they died, what happened?"

"My bushes are all dead! I even put that dry fertilizer right on the roots when I planted them . . ."

Back in Florida, when I was selling wholesale to florists, we once had a customer who looked over an order of pink poinsettias we had set in back of her store and then ask with concern, "Are these going to get any redder?"–from Chris Beytes (Grower Talks)

Customer: "Is this plant gonna die?"

Clerk: "If it's God's will…"

From our world famous rose gardens in Portland, OR, Harry the Rosemeister told this story:

I worked retail some years ago and we once had a woman come in and buy a slew of boxed roses, you know the ones with the big color picture on the side? She came back a month later and demanded her money back. Well, we weren't going to pay 'til we saw that $300 planting of roses. So we came by her place (I'll leave the first part last) and we saw soil that was beautifully tilled and amended. We then saw a drip irrigation system, perfect for not getting water on the foliage… Oh? The first part? She had planted all 20 roses upside down. Her reason – she wanted to see what color they were.

SOME
STORIES
AND A
BLESSING

CUTE STORIES

Sweetness: When five-year-old Sarah Cooperman came up to her mother with a hug (after her mom was mucking the garden with manure), she took a big inhale and said, "Oh, Mommy, you smell like a garden before the flowers are born."

British four-year-old Timmy Miller was looking forward to a new brother or sister. The time for the "birds and bees" talk was imminent. His mother explained, "Daddy planted a seed in me and in nine months' time, you will have a new brother or sister!" Timmy fell into deep thought,". . . Mummy?"
"Yes, dear…"
"When I was grown, was my face on the seed packet?"

A customer came into the garden center asking for "salivas." Our clerk politely asked if she meant "*Salvia*," to which the customer insisted it was saliva she was after. The clerk showed her to the annuals section and helped her pick out a couple of nice 4" Salvia plants. Then the customer asked what would look nice with her saliva (again). Unable to resist the temptation, the clerk said, "Well, I think your nice saliva would really look good with some 'spitoonias'."

"The Dirt Nazi"

Most Seinfeld fans remember the Soup Nazi–that nasty New York City restaurateur that wouldn't serve customers unless they followed his rules precisely. I'd like to tell you about someone whom my wife, my in-laws and I have known as the Dirt Nazi.

The Dirt Nazi and his wife run a North Texas garden center. It's a typical mom-and-pop store that sells a decent variety of plants, but is probably best known for its bulk goods. They have fabulous compost and mulches and I've hauled dozens of truck-loads and flatbed-trailer loads out of that place over the years. The Dirt Nazi is in his late 50s, built like a Portapotty and wears overalls and a pith helmet. He's a sullen man with a permanent frown, who speaks in a low grumble. But he'd prefer never to speak to anybody. Mrs. Dirt Nazi is a friendly, chipper little sprite. (I don't know how she puts up with him.)

The Dirt Nazi earned his name one Saturday morning. My wife and I pulled in around 8:45 and walked into the store. He screamed at us to get out and said, "Everybody in town knows that we haven't opened until 9 o'clock on Saturday in 20 years!"

How silly of us. We should have ignored the open gate and the sign on his window that said, "Open." So we drove around the block a few times and went back in.

Once in early fall I showed up and the place was devoid of other customers. I requested a half yard of compost and the Dirt Nazi asked, "How strong are you?" "Strong enough to unload a half yard of compost," I responded. Emotionless, he said, "Come with me," and he led me to an old poly greenhouse where a gas unit heater sat on a bench. "Help me lift this so my wife can bolt it up to the trusses." So he and I hoisted this heater up–(it must have weighed 300 pounds) while Mrs. Dirt Nazi tried to attach the thing to the wooden beams about seven feet off the ground. By the time she got the nuts started, the Dirt Nazi and I were red faced, groaning like Russian power lifters, and about to blow blood vessels in our temples.

He didn't say thank you, and he didn't give me a discount, but he did say he'd give me a little extra compost for my troubles. For him, that meant not shaking the excess compost from the top of the half-yard bucket of his skid steer before dumping it into my truck bed.

Thanks, Dirt Nazi. You're the king of customer service!

-- *Todd Davis, Editor, "Nursery Management & Production"*

God Was Overheard Talking To St. Francis

God: Frank, you know all about gardens and nature. What in the world is going on down there with those humans? What happened to the dandelions, violets, thistles and stuff I started eons ago? I had a perfect, no-maintenance garden plan. Those plants grow in any type of soil, withstand drought and multiply with abandon. The nectar from the long-lasting blossoms attract butterflies, honeybees and flocks of songbirds. I expected to see a vast garden of colors by now. But all I see are these green rectangles.

St. Francis: It's the tribe that settled there, Lord. The Suburbanites. They started calling your flowers "weeds" and went to great extent to kill them and replace them with grass.

God: Grass? But it's so boring. It's not colorful. It doesn't attract butterflies, birds and bees, only grubs and sod worms. It's temperamental with temperatures. Do these Suburbanites really want all that grass growing there?

St. Francis: Apparently so, Lord. They go to great pains to grow it and keep it green. They begin each spring by fertilizing grass and poisoning any other plant that crops up in the lawn.

God: The Suburbanites must be happy that the spring rains and cool weather make grass grow really fast.

St. Francis: Apparently not, Lord. As soon as it grows a little, they cut it, sometimes twice a week.

God: They cut it?   Do they then bail it like hay?

St. Francis: Not exactly Lord. Most of them rake it up and put it in bags.

God: They bag it? Why? Is it a cash crop? Do they sell it?

St. Francis: No, sir. Just the opposite. They pay to throw it away.

God: Now let me get this straight. They fertilize grass so it will grow. And when it does grow, they cut it off and pay to throw it away?

St. Francis: Yes, sir.

God: These Suburbanites must be relieved when we slow down the growth of plants. That surely saves them a lot of work.

St. Francis: You aren't going to believe this, Lord. When the grass stops growing so fast, they drag out hoses and pay more money to water it so they can continue to mow it and pay to get rid of it.

God: What nonsense! At least they kept the trees. That was a sheer stroke of genius, if I do say so myself. The trees grow leaves in the spring to provide beauty and shade in the summer. In the autumn they fall to the ground and form a natural blanket to keep moisture in the soil and protect the trees and bushes. It's a natural circle of life.

St. Francis: You'd better sit down, Lord. The Suburbanites have drawn a new circle. As soon as the leaves fall, they rake them into great piles and have them hauled away.

God: No! What do they do to protect the shrub and tree roots in the winter and keep the soil moist and loose?

St. Francis: After throwing away your leaves, they go out and buy something they call mulch. They haul it home and spread it around in place of the leaves.

God: And where do they get this mulch?

St. Francis: They cut down trees and grind them up.

God: Enough! I don't want to think about this anymore. St. Catherine, you're in charge of the arts. What movie have you scheduled for us tonight?

St. Catherine: Dumb and Dumber, Lord. It's a really stupid movie about...

God: Never mind, I think I just heard the whole story.

A Gardener's Blessing

May the bunnies never nibble
on your young and tender shoots,
May your transplants settle in
and put down hardy roots,
May your weeds come out real easy
and your lawn be fungus free,
May you never put your back out
or inhale a bumblebee,
May your roses never stab you
or your hoses spring a leak,
And may everyone come calling
when your garden's at its peak,
May you never grow too weary
as you toil for hours and hours,
And may you never be too busy
to stop and smell the flowers!

SIGNS, STUDENTS, & ROOKIES

SIGNS

Portapotties at a nursery were labeled Dictamnus *and* Sagina

Sign in a garden center: "We guarantee our plants until they are in your car."

A totally beat-up landscaper's pickup truck in a garden center parking lot carried the proud sign, "Press on Regardless."

STUDENTS

John "Greenfingers" Colwill, an Australian garden consultant and teacher, shared this list of exam mistakes from horticulture students:

- "Spray tanks should always be filled with adequate protective clothing."

- On Brussels sprout harvesting: "This system is not too popular with workers who don't enjoy stripping outside in all weather."

- "Annuals die once a year, biennials twice a year, but perennials go on forever."

- "If workers keep hoeing weeds during a dry summer, most of them will eventually die."

- "In January, don't do any culvaticus until February."

- "Always take blackcurrant cuttings from blackcurrant bushes."

- "Fish should be kept in ponds to keep them from turning green."

- "French marigolds mixed with saliva make a good summer bedding scheme."

- "When using poisonous sprays, be sure to have the right anecdote ready!"

ROOKIES!

Once, a customer brought a leaf covered with insects into the garden center and wanted to know what they were. The clerk told him they were "baby aphids." I saw them-they were actually scale (lots of them in the crawler stage). Anyway, we laughed about the baby aphids for a long time.

One day a man and his Asian wife approached one of our newest cashiers. He said that he needed a "China boy for his China girl," which caught our employee totally off guard. She recovered and referred them to a salesperson, who showed the customer where the male *Ilex* pollinators were located.

A few years ago we had a new employee who was still learning about our various products. When a customer asked if we had any purple martin houses, our new-hire replied, "No, but we have some green and white ones."

Sales clerk: "We call these perennial-annuals."

Student: "It's more like landscape archi-torture!"

Customer asked for flags-the young clerk sent her to a hardware store.

BAD
LATIN
&
QUOTES

Irate customer upon hearing a Latin name, exclaimed," I don't do *those* names . . . I need the **real** names!" [From Becky Dean]

A British customer came into a NW nursery and said she wanted a *Penis contorta*.[*Pinus* is pronounced "penis" in Europe].

Not long ago, my friend and fellow Canadian, Cindy, was speaking with her friend in the U.S. about her fondness for the Eastern redbud. When she used the botanical name, Cindy's friend interrupted her. "*Cercis canadensis*" wouldn't apply to me, dear." She said seriously. "*I'm* an American."

"Do you have enemas for a ground cover?" [*Euonymus*–Dan]

Sophisticated customer, "I'd like some *Leucanthemum* 'Macaroni'…" [*Leucanthemum* 'Marconi'–Dan]

We also like to joke around at work about some of the Latin names– for instance, there is this shrub called summersweet, whose Latin name is *Clethra* and suggest a combination with *Gunnera*. So we say, "Has your *Clethra* got *Gunnera*?"

Customer: "I'd like a japonica."

Dan Heims spoke at the Chicago Botanic Garden. After touring the city and seeing seas of yews, he climbed atop an imaginary soap-box, struck a political pose, and promised, "NO NEW TAXUS!"

Customer: "I'd like an *Erocticum* 'Bill Heron'." [*Erodium*–heronsbill–Dan]

Customer: "I'd like a 7-foot tall *Crocus*" [*Quercus* or oak–Dan]

Do you have any *Achillea* 'Moonshot'? ['Moonbeam' –Dan]

Dan Hinkley was asked if he had made the "transition" from *Zauschneria* to *Epilobium*. He responded, "No way! I just learned how to **spell** *Zauschneria*!"

"*Peeina* 'Bowl of Beauty'? That's the Latin, right?
Sure it is.   I just love learning the Latin because I've read that
gardeners all over the world will know what I mean when I name a
plant. No more of this peony for me, no way. "
[*Paeonia lactiflora* 'Bowl of Beauty']

Dan spoke at the Far West show in Portland, Oregon on
landscaping and was asked why he didn't use Crabapples (which
are mildew-prone there) Dan replied, "We prefer to have *Malus*
towards none. . ."   *rim tap*

"Does the white-flowered *Mazus* attract snakes?"

"What exactly is a **Helleborus**? I have been reading about them."

"How do you spell the scientific name of bellworts?"

A young, eager new employee was trying to learn botanical Latin
and mispronounced several names in a row. He groaned, threw
his hands in the air and said, "Everyone's going to think I went to
Densiformis Yew!"

But are they
100% Vinly?

"I have a rock garden. Last week, three of them died."
– [Richard Diran]

A perennial is a plant that would have come back year after year had it survived.

The best way to garden is to put on a wide-brimmed straw hat and some old clothes. And with a hoe in one hand and a cold drink in the other, tell somebody else where to dig.
– [Texas Bix Bender, Don't Throw in the Trowel]

Ketzel Levine of "Talking Plants" defines "bottomist" as:
"a botanist with their head in flowers and their butt in the air."

If you are not killing plants, you are not really stretching yourself as a gardener.

Gardening requires lots of water–most of it in the form of perspiration.– [Lou Erickson]

What a man needs in gardening is a cast-iron back,. . .
with a hinge in it.– [Charles Dudley Warner]

Heard from a fellow female greenhouse manager, complimenting her colleague's work, "You grow, girl!"

Eschewing all perennials for ferns, Judith Jones let out, "With fronds like these, who needs anemones?"

POETRY
FOR
PLANTOPHILES

The Nurseryman's Prayer

The nurseryman stood at the golden gate,
His head was bent and low.
He merely asked the man of fate,
Which way he ought to go.
"What have you done?" St. Peter said,
"To seek admittance here. . ."
"I ran a nursery down on earth,
For many and many a year."
St. Peter opened wide the gate,
And gently pressed the bell.
"Come in!" he said, "and choose your harp,"
"You've had your share of hell."

–*Euonymus* (From Matt Gardiner)

Why Did My Plant Die?
–Geoffrey B. Charlesworth

You walked too close, you trod on it.

You dropped a piece of sod on it.

You hoed it down. You weeded it.

You planted it the wrong way up,

You grew it in a yogurt cup.

You forgot to make a hole;

The soggy compost took its toll.

September storm, November drought.

It heaved in March–its roots popped out.

You covered it with herbicide.

You scattered bone meal far and wide,

Attracting local omnivores,

Who ate your plant, and stayed for more.

You left it baking in the sun,

While you departed in a run.

To find a spade, perhaps a trowel.

You planted it with crown too high;

The soil washed off, that explains why.

Too high pH. It hated lime.

Alas it needs a gentler clime.

You left the root ball wrapped in plastic.

You broke the roots–they're not elastic.

You walked too close, you trod on it.

You dropped a piece of sod on it.

You splashed the plant with mower oil.
You should do something to the soil.
Too rich. Too poor. Such wretched tilth.
Your soil is clay. Your soil is filth.
Your plant was eaten by a slug.
The growing point contained a bug.
The aphids are controlled by ants,
Who milk the juice. It kills the plants.
In early spring, your garden's mud.
You walked around! That's not much good.
With heat and light, you hurried it.
You worried it, you buried it.
The poor plant missed the mountain air;
No heat, no summer muggs up there.
You overfed it ten-ten-ten.
You forgot to water it again.
You hit it sharply with a hose,
You used a can without a rose.
Perhaps you sprinkled from above.
You should have talked to it with love.
The nursery mailed it without the roots.
You killed it with those gardening boots.
You walked too close, you trod on it.
You dropped a piece of sod on it.

To

My

Garden

Hose

Joan Norton,
Betty's Bay
Australia

I wish I loved you, Garden Hose!
You are an asset, I suppose;
My garden would most surely fail,
Were water carried by a pail.
But oh! How you can make me curse,
Fret and fume, and write this verse!

Each time you cross a garden bed,
A favorite blossom you behead.
Pulling you around from place to place,
There's not a thing you won't embrace:
Bump of brick and spike of log,
Leg of bench and bowl of dog.
And if no obstacles exist,
You knot yourself with kink and twist.
I give a flick to set you free–
You hook up on the nearest tree!

Across my garden path at night,
You trip me up with great delight.
And every single chance you get,
You do your best to make me wet.
With jet and dribble, leak, and squirt,
You soak my shoes and spray my skirt.
Your sprinkler sticks – I set it free–
At once, you shoot all over me!

Oh garden serpent, I believe
The ancient enmity of Eve
Exists between us, as of yore:
We'll live in hate forevermore.

Oh how I bless the rainy day,
When I can coil you away!

HORTIHOLICS
ANONYMOUS

You Might Be A Hortiholic ...

- If you haul home bushel baskets-full of cow manure or bark in the trunk of your Mercedes sports coupe.

- If instead of hiding receipts from Nordstrom's like all of your friends, you hope your spouse won't find the (insert any expensive nursery name) charges!

- If it rains, you think, "Good, that makes it easier to pull weeds."

- If the plant tag says "rare" you buy it, even if you don't have a place for it.

- If it rains, you think, "All right! I don't have to hand water all of those pots today."

- If you have a rare and beautiful day in February you feel *compelled* to spend the day either: at a nursery, working in the garden, or just wandering the garden looking to see what wonderful things are popping their heads up!

[Zone 7 writer –Dan]

- If the first thing you read in the Sunday paper is the gardening section.

- If the Flower and Garden Show is on your calendar a year in advance.

- If your favorite piece of mail for the year is the Heronswood catalog.

- If you subscribe to every gardening–related magazine.

- If, even though your shelves are full of books on gardening, you cannot resist one more.

- If you go on vacation, you miss your garden.

- If you decide NOT to go on vacation because it is the best time in your garden!

- If you realize you cannot move because you can't take all your beloved plants with you.

- If you go to New York City and all you can think of is how do I get to Wave Hill and the Brooklyn Botanical Garden?

- If you buy a house based solely on the "possibilities" the garden has to offer, not on the house itself.

- If your friends are grouped into "gardener" and "non-gardener" categories.

- If you hope your child grows up to be a gardener. Who needs a doctor in the family?

- If you agree to go with your spouse to the hardware store only if it carries gardening supplies.

- If you take leaf or stem cuttings from plants at the local garden center with the excuse that you are using the leaf for plant identification (this is without purchasing the plant).

- If your idea of fun is to try to identify all the trees you drive past along the highway.

- If you always have a huge collection (in your driveway) of plants waiting to be planted.

- If you are out for a Sunday drive in the Model A Ford with your wife and mother-in-law, swing into the local nursery, and buy so many plants that mom has to ride home in the rumble seat.

- If you never leave the garden center without writing *at least* two checks (so true!).

- If you look at any bare patch of ground and start a mental landscape design.

- If you pot up all the stray seedlings in your garden and find them good homes.

- If you cancelled a spa appointment to hear a special speaker at the plant society meeting.

- If you have to leave not one car, but both, out of the garage over winter because it's full of tender dormant plants.

- If walking through a crowded park with your teenage children, you spot a recently cut *Juniperus virginiana*. To the horror of your kids, you bend over and smell the aromatic stump, and squeal how wonderful it is.

Real Gardeners ...

- squish "bad" bugs (or slugs) with their bare hands
- actually spend money on a sack of poop
- give advice to other customers at garden centers
- stop on the way home from buying plants
  — to buy more plants
- will, within five minutes of entering someone else's garden, start pulling weeds.
- find seeds falling off plants and into their hands when they visit other gardens
- can be recognized from May to September by a telltale hint of dirt under their fingernails
- know what *Taraxacum officinale* is
- have gardens that are never finished
- keep an "emergency gardening kit" in the trunk of their car
- can always find room for just *one more*!

You Know You're A Plant Nerd When ...

A skit performed by Dan Heims and Dawn Hummel
at Plant Nerd Night, in Portland, OR, 2003

You know you're a plant nerd when ...
You go out at night with a flashlight to show your friends your latest plant acquisition.

You know you're a plant nerd when ...
It takes two years to grow a flippin' blue poppy, and you take photos to record this magical feat. Then, your partner deletes the digital photos and you threaten to kill or divorce him or her.

You know you're a plant nerd when ...
You drive back from a garden show with so many plants in the car, you can't see out the window (ANY of them!)

You know you're a plant nerd when ...
You receive more gardening magazines than you can ever read, so you start a personal library in the bathroom.

You know you're a plant nerd when ...
You go to Starbucks and instead of ordering a mocha, you order coffee grounds for your compost bin–to go.

You know you're a plant nerd when ...
You partner looks at you in disgust as you throw icky compost around the garden with your bare hands and you smile back while exclaiming, "But, it's gold, honey!"

You know you're a plant nerd when ...
You interrupt a slideshow when viewing a totally cool new plant and doing this:
[*Dan–thrusts up his bic® lighter and shouts. . "Oh Yeah!!!"]*
[*Or the women's version, "O-MY-GOD!"]*

You know you're a plant nerd when ...
Your friends eat a pile of hazelnuts and you look at the shells and say, "You done with those?"
[*We use them as mulch in Oregon–Dan]*

You know you're a plant nerd when ...
The sounds coming from the lecture hall sound like a fireworks display.
[*Dawn: "OOH! Aah, Oooh!"]*

[*set up chairs with fake steering wheel]*

You know you're a plant nerd when ...
You nearly kill your passengers when you see a cool plant off to the side of the road.

You know you're a plant nerd when ...

Planning for a flower show sounds more like a military operation:

> Protein bars – check!
> Bottled water – yup!
> Digital camera – righttio!
> Cell phone/Walkie Talkie – *"double flowering hellebores on aisle 1500! HURRY!"*
> Speaker schedule – check!
> Money – lots!
> Credit cards – which ones?! All of 'em.
> Luggage carrier – yes!
> Garden outfit – ta da!

Stance of a drill sergeant with a clipboard, all props on stage

[The skit continues at a piano–Dawn playing, and Dan alternating
lines and singing in an Archie Bunker take-off]

Those Were the Days

All the plants for which we've paid,
Plants you've broken with your spade,
Gard'ning was our stock and trade,
those were the days,
And the plant names you knew when,
They like to change them now and then,
Mister we could use a man like that Linnaeus again,
So let's go out and grab a rake,
All those weeds we'll overtake,
Gee, our lawn mower ran great,
Those were the days!

The Hortiholic Twelve–Step Program

[Dawn and Dan showing somber, though determined faces]

"Hi I'm Dan Heims ...and I'm Dawn Hummel and we're **BOTH**
Hortiholics.

We have formulated a twelve–step program to help all of you who
share in our addiction:"

1. We admit that we are powerless over buying plants–that our
purchases have depleted and continue to deplete our
savings.

2. We have come to believe that a Power greater than ourselves
could control the "flor-gasms" we continually have in public.

3. We remove our license plate holder that says,
"Warning, I brake for plant sales!"

44

4. We try to remember the 3 C's:

- I **C**an't control it

- I **C**an't cure it

- and I surely didn't **C**ause it
  [Thank you, Kelly Dodson]

5. We have learned the error of our ways,
after we have planted 20 variegated plants together.

6. We will learn to control our plant passions through–
raise 2 trowels: "Trowel and Error"

7. We fall into the depths of denial when we:

A. Can't afford them;

B. Don't have room for them;

C. Can't grow them in this zone;

D. And we still buy them anyway.

8. We beg forgiveness every time we break our partner's
favorite tool.

9. We vow to use common names in front of non-plant nerds
whenever possible. (or simply admit that we are all
"Latin Lovers")

10. We will continue to take inventory of our "staging areas"
and REMEMBER that integration is KEY before the partner
comes home.

11. We will justify the purchase of all kinds of hardscaping to
improve the value of our homes.

12 We vow not to buy more plants than we can carry . . .
to the holding area of the Hardy Plant Society sale.

ODDS
&
ENDS

ODDS AND ENDS

My wife sent me here for some aphrodisiacs, Aphrodites? [arborvitaes?—Dan]

Heard from Raymond Evison, the clematis expert, to a woman who said her clematis wouldn't grow: "Try putting some old cow manure on it!" The sage advice was met by darting eyes accusing him of losing his senses. "Now, where am I going to find an old cow in this area?" she haughtily replied.

Another from U.K. broadcaster, Alan Titchmarsh, who told of a woman who complained about her roses being so tall that she couldn't reach the flowers: His advice of "Give it the occasional prune", was met several weeks later by the woman calling up and saying, "It's had half a tin of prunes now and it still doesn't seem to be improving!"

Innocently, from a young female customer to a male clerk: "Do you have the balls for gazing?"

A laborer who worked with me once called me a "Horticardiologist."

A young summer kid said that sycamore trees in bloom look like "giant alyssum."

"This garden is so photogenetic!"

One customer insisted that she wanted "jupiters." She had planted them at all her previous houses and had had good luck with them. After referring to them as junipers several times during our conversation, I gave up and sold her the jupiters. Couldn't find any other planets to give her a complete solar system though.

Customer: "Where is your red hot poker?"
Blushing young male clerk: "In the front, ma'am."

From a Home Depot clerk: A woman came into our garden department looking to buy some halogen bulbs that her husband wanted!

While admiring a lovely *Zauschneria* (a California plant with orange flowers), Baldassare Mineo, of Siskiyou Rare Plant Nursery, said, "Dan, don't you know that orange is the new pink?"

After reviewing the trial fields at Terra Nova Nurseries, a customer smiled and said, "This is the beginning of a beautiful obsession!"

The favorite request I heard when I worked the Chicago Botanic Garden plant sale was when someone asked where the "phonies" were—meaning peonies. I laughed for days!

Three definitions heard at a garden center:
      Arcade: the structure you grow flowers on
      Evergreen: everlasting plants
      Perennials : these are the ones that make a full cycle

Ron Bayer, the owner of the largest nursery in St. Louis, once told me a funny one about a lady wanting to buy 'Golden Vicary' Privet. He told her that they carried them in 1-gallon, 3-gallon, and 5-gallon. She responded, astonished, "It's a liquid???"

Dan Heims attended a propagator's conference in Portland, OR and the speaker was talking about doing "high-grafts" on Bradford Pears (*Pyrus calleryana*), also called the "Callery pear". When question time came about, Dan asked, "Why don't you do a low graft?" The speaker looked at him like he was from outer space and snorted, "Why would I *ever* want to do that?" Dan replied, "So you can have a low Callery pear!"

A customer once asked, "Do you carry "macho pine"?"

At Powell's Bookstore in Portland, a gardener asked for Karen Platt's *Black Magic and Purple Passion* (a book on dark leaved plants) and was sent to the erotica section.

A customer called Midwest Groundcovers some years ago with the question, "How tall is Miss Kim?" My answer was, "She's about four feet." The caller replied, "I was asking about the plant, not the person."

The female keeper of the shade greenhouse at Portland Nursery was titled the "Princess of Darkness".

In front of a huge pansy display a customer asked, "Which are the winter pansies?" [They *all* are!—Dan]

Dave Schultz remembers asking his crew to bring up a dozen 5 gallon *Cortaderia* from the field and was met by puzzled looks. Fortunately a wise crew member piped up, "Oh, he means the 'cut-yuh-up' plants!" Brief nods were seen all around, and the plants were immediately pulled.

Several years ago a customer brought in a plant purchased from Home Depot and wondered what it was. She really wanted to know, and for a year or so we referred to it as "the Home Depot plant." Finally *Angelonia* became widely grown and we realized that's what she had.

"I practice "cramscaping!"

A Real Conversation. . .

R ed rum, do you have any here?
Garden Clerk: Do you mean the . . .
Customer: I would like the red rum, you know, big red rum leaves.
GC: Okay, think I know what you want. Do you want an eating variety? or the ornamental?
C: Hell, I don't know, I just want the red rum; I'll take that one over there.
GC: Well actually, that's a colocasia, not a rum, a *Rheum*, I mean.
C: That one is a what? Not a *Rheum*, rum I mean?
GC: No, that's what some folks call elephant ears, but it's a beautiful foliage plant.
C: Now, what has that got to do with red rum? Elephant ears? Is that a new kind of rum?
GC: No, not at all, it's another type of plant altogether. Are you sure you have your heart set on the red rum? If not, I'm sure you'd love the *Colocasia*.
C: I really, really want the red rum, that one over there.[the colocasia].
GC: No problem, you'll love it. Just remember to take it in for the winter; it's not hardy here. And you won't be able to eat it like ordinary rhubarb, since it's not in the rhubarb family.
C: Who said anything about rhubarb? I just wanted this red rum here; it's just like my neighbor has. We sit around in his yard most nights and have a bit of toddy and he calls that plant his red rum. Gotcha good this time, lady!
GC: Yup, he sure did.

[*Rheum palmatum* var. 'Atrosanguineum' and *Colocasia*—Dan]

Have you ever heard of arboritis?
No, is it a disease?
No, they're evergreen bushes people plant in front of their houses.
[*Arborvitae*—Dan]

"I would buy some of your lilies, but I already have my flowers the way I want them this year."

Several of us spent considerable time one spring helping a customer looking for "the pink shrub blooming everywhere now." It turned out to be groundcover phlox.

I am always amused by the many gardeners who come in every spring and ask my help in finding "you know, what I planted last year!"

Dick and Judith Tyler are hellebore breeders who call themselves "hellawhores."

That plant is so sensitive – it could get shade burn!

Many years ago, before I knew about *Viburnum plicatum* (Shasta and others) I was driving in a remote wooded area with many of them in bloom. I stopped at a house and inquired, "What are these beautiful white flowering shrubs?" The little lady replied, "Tame dogwoods."

Man and wife approaching supermarket with hanging baskets outside:
He "Honey, is this what you are looking for?"
She "No! I want the kind you don't have to water."

Customer asked for abortives and wanted arborvitaes.
Another one called to talk to an arborist and asked for an abortionist.

"I like flowers that don't bloom"

From one of our more seasoned gardeners:
A young reporter at a horticultural expo rushed up to the
beautiful dark haired movie actress and asked, "How long have
you been a gardener, Ava?"

"I bought my petunias here last week. I came back to see what kind
of dirt you got."

Small town garden writer tells of her tour of an Arboretum—and
her excitement regarding a large tree—"as I turned the corner, I
was struck by a 25-foot tree."

Barbara Bush's staff member called and complained about Walter's Gardens plant: *Leucanthemum super**bum*** 'Barbara Bush'.

Customer to a landscape designer: "I'd like plants, you know.... different ones of different heights."

(From Michelle) Here are some of my special requests from customers at a retail store that I work in:

green peckers–need I say more
dripping hearts
hostages–hostas
hollycocks–hollyhocks...This was from a little old lady who
        wanted the ground to open up as soon as she uttered it.
daffy's dil–daffodil bulbs
peeping jenny–creeping jenny
ammonia–anemone
bearded tongue–beardtongue
doglilies–daylilies
violets–violas
foxes–phlox
potentillers–potentillas...The lady commented that she had just
finished her rototilling and was looking for some potentillers
cat chow/catmint—I told her that the cat food was in the pet
department. She had a shocked reaction on her face and so I asked
if she wanted cat chow or catmint. Realizing her faux pas, she
laughed and said catmint will be fine.
black-eyed peas–black eyed-Susans
cotton easters–cotoneasters
flea baths–flea bane
Chrys anty moms–chrysanthemums
weedwhackers–weedtrimmers

"My Monrovia maple died!" [Monrovia puts all of their offerings in pots with their name on it–Dan]

Heard on a nursery speaker, "Does anybody in back have a sweet box?" Not hearing the chortling, the announcer continued, "It's a woody...." [*Sarcococca*–Dan]

Customer: "I'd like a stik-stake tomato."[Stik-stake was a brand of label –Dan]

"I am having a terrible time finding *my* scarlet sage this year!"

When working my way through college, I worked weekends at a K-Mart™ Garden Center. About 200 potted azaleas hadn't been watered for several weeks and were dead. I asked the manager if I should throw them away. He said, "No, mark them down to $1.00 a piece." I told him I was going to tell everyone who wanted to buy one that they were dead and wouldn't grow. He said, "Ok." I told everyone who brought one of the azaleas to the front counter that they were dead. We sold every one of them. The common comment was, "What can I lose for just one dollar?" I realized I didn't know much about marketing.... or human nature. (Carol Wallace)

Customer: "I'd like an Ogilvee Geranium" [Ogilvee, an international plant breeder, has many varieties–Dan]

Customer remarking on a store's great variety of plants: "My, you've got quite a menage-a-trois!"

Is this plant a perennial? (alternately pre-ennial?) [Yes, we've heard this more than once.]
Yes, it is.
Oh. I won't get it then. I prefer plants that come back every year.

"I would like one of those spotted hostas." [*Pulmonaria*–Dan]

Paw paw tree pronounced, papa tree. A garden center owner actually said this! If it bears fruit, does that make it a mama tree?

From Minnesota: "Do you have lotsa hotsa? I'm a hotsa nut.
I'd like to meet some other hotsa nuts; I collect them."
"Really?"
"Oh ya, I must have at least thirty of them in pots, you know, and
in the winter I kinda like to think they like it in the cellar. Most of
them have still been alive and ready to go in the spring. You know,
it's just kinda like they can't wait to get outside.

Customer looking at Dwarf Pineapple plant in tropical collection:
"What is that on top?!"
GC:"A pineapple."
C:"Oh, my God! I had no idea pineapples grew on plants!"

Hackberry pronounced as "heckleberry." I actually heard this
used by a professional forester while we were discussing native
plants. He worked for a conservation authority and he regarded
himself as an expert. Does that mean that somewhere nearby there
is "jeckleberry"?

Female Customer: Do you have any naked ladies? [*Lycoris
squamigera*–Dan]
Male clerk: No, but the day ain't over yet.
[Yes, this really happened–Debbie]

While working at Waterford Gardens, we actually had a customer
ask, "Are water lilies plants or animals?"

A friend who works for a company that sells interior plants often
gets asked for "fiscus" or, more fun, "fuc_us" trees.

"Could you direct me to the paper*weight* Narcissus?"

Noelle heard people requesting red-hot weenie, red-hot cat tail, and
flaming hot dog plant, applied to the chenille plant, *Acalypha hispida*.

These ferns I bought here, there's bugs that grew on the back and I can't cut them off! [spore cases –Dan]

Gary Vanburen awarded his best bulb customers with a ball of aged gouda with a mottled wax exterior as a Christmas gift.
Sure enough, one of his customers called back six months later and shouted,"Gary! That damn bulb you gave me–it never came up!"

I was a rookie intern working at Kurt Bluemel's greenhouse. I was given the arduous job of labeling an extensive collection of grass stock plants, creating very large labels. Kurt's laugh was heard several blocks away when he saw the huge label I made, reading
Miscanthus 'Don T. Cut'   [don't cut–Dan]

My favorite story came from Lynn Cohen who had spent years working at Behnke's Nursery in Maryland. She was called from her desk to help on "the floor" and met this anxious and well-dressed man...
Lynn: "May I help you?"
Man: "Uh, yes, my wife told me to pick up some chlamydia."
Lynn (surely blushing): "Uh, perhaps she meant Clematis–a vine with purple flowers?"
Man: (raising voice) "She said CLAH-mydia"
Lynn: "Perhaps she wanted *Campanula,* a low groundcover?"
Man: (flustered) "Is there a REAL nurseryman here?"
Lynn: (indignantly) "Sir! I have more experience than anyone here and I know darn well that chlamydia is a venereal disease. If you'd like to get that, I can recommend a topless bar down the street!"
Man: (sheepishly) "Oh man, You're going to talk about me for the rest of the week..."
Lynn: (laughing) "No, sir, I'll be talking about you for the rest of my LIFE!"

Around Mother's Day we get a few calls from older customers asking for "high geraniums." What they want are florist hydrangeas.

Once a customer walked up to me and asked me with a completely straight face, "You got any Cannabis?"
"Cannabis?" I said.
"Yep, Cannabis." I tried hard not to laugh while I tried to figure out what plant this person wanted. I finally figured out she wanted a canna lily. Somebody had a good time during the 60s.

As per your request in the July/August issue of *Garden Design*, following are some beauties I enjoyed during the eighteen years I owned and operated Pine Tree Nursery & Garden Center on Cape Cod in South Chatham, MA.

There were frequent requests for "prostate junipers", "yellow margaritas", "white asylum", "blue saliva" and "black-eyed lazy Susans."

Overheard in the nursery: "I'm looking for a straight plant called 'Gay Feather'."

And joking at the check-out counter: "I thought I was going to have a sweet pea but ended up taking a leek." [everyone's a comedian! –Dan]

A married older couple, both avid gardeners, conspired against one another. Every season they would come in and individually confide in us. He'd lean over the counter and say, "She keeps buying plants, so I must dig more holes!" So he would buy soil and fertilizers and put them into the car. Then she would come in and puff, "He keeps digging holes, so I must buy more plants!" And so she would make her selections and take them to the car. Then they would get into the car and drive off together.

A landscape laborer in his third season of performing spring cleanups anticipated the tedious job of hand–removing lots of leaves from a large bed of *Cotoneaster horizontalis*. On alighting from his truck he inquired of the customer, "Are you gonna have us clean up all those cotonee-pain-in-the-asters?"

Using common names for plants can always get you in trouble, and so can using incorrect terminology. Snatches of conversations overheard at the local garden club monthly teas could surely raise eyebrows: Did I really hear... talk of "naked ladies," rumors of "Johnny jumps around," requests for "touch-me-not" and tittering about "dizzy Lizzie"? Were there mutterings about cutting off "mother-in-law's tongue" and sighs about stroking "lamb's tongue," whispers of "deflowering heather," and of seeing "Miss Willmott's Ghost"?

Who's On First? came to life for me when I was consulting with a customer about refurbishing her landscape after a particularly hard winter. As we went through our ideas for replacements the customer kept saying, "skip hollies" so I asked why, as there were several on the property that were doing well. Her response was "because we like them." So I'd suggest them when the next opportunity arrived, and she'd repeat, "skip hollies." After several repetitions of this conversation we arrived at a corner of the garden where there resided two gorgeous specimen "Shipke holly." I finally understood what my tongue-tied customer was trying to say and we subsequently planted for her several new "Skip" hollies, as they had come to be known.

Once a customer asked me if I had a margarita. I was thinking no, but I wished I did. Upon further questioning, I realized she wanted a marguerite daisy. It's not nice to tease people that way.

And I presume gardening snobs are "horti-toity"?

Some of my favorites are things people have said at the nursery, and many are plant requests or questions about the plants. One went like this: "My husband's hot poker died last week. Do you have any in stock I could put in today?" [*Kniphofia*–Dan]

A nursery customer brought back a plant for full credit because she thought there were "piles" of slug eggs on the surface. The clerk gently informed her that this was a fertilizer called Osmocote®!

"They ought to call it hortiTORTURE!"–Cindy Gilberg

I decided this summer that they have named varieties of coleus after porn stars. How else can you explain names like 'Hurricane Louise', 'Japanese Giant', 'Inky Fingers' and 'Giant Fantasy'?

*I love the customers who come up to me and ask
"Do you work here?"—I'm usually in uniform and dirty!*

"Is it okay to continue to use Miracle Whip™ on my plants all season?"

Stuck for a good term for annuals, the official map of the Prague Botanical Garden has an area labeled "Perennials and dying plants."

Customer looking at an *Arborvitae*, "Now, I don't have this exact model, but it's similar."

Several years ago I worked for a garden center in Utah. The owner grew fresh produce also. Tom and Linda came in and Tom wanted some hot peppers for salsa. I said try the 'Cherry Bomb' and I'll pay for it if you eat it. He put the whole pepper in his mouth. His wife asked how it was. Tom, in a very low voice and with a grim face, said, "HOT!"
Linda asked, "Do I still need to make salsa?" Tom, again in a very low voice said, "YES!" So Linda went to buy some Cherry Bombs and Tom took out the 'Cherry Bombs' and put in some bell peppers in the basket. So I guess he burned his mouth so bad that he just wanted mild salsa! I bought the pepper for Tom!

"I need a hooka; I'd like one for the weekend. I really like the big ones." [*Heuchera*–Dan]"

"I'd like a Hepissapile-a"
"Okay, which kind would you like?"
"The yellow."
"Well, that is a good choice."
[*Heliopsis helianthoides* 'Gigantea'– only one color in the genus–Dan]

Several times each year, either from our retail or internet customers, we will have requests for a variety named 'Prostrate' rosemary, but invariably someone will always want the "prostate" rosemary, because they want their husband or father to maintain their health! We always explain the misunderstanding, but sometimes it just doesn't matter.

I'd sure like to find hootchorella; I'd love one of them with the white bloomers. I forgot, is it 'Bridget'? Whatever, I'd take 'Bridget' with the bloomers. If you don't have any of the white, I'll take one with the red bottoms, I mean bloomers, flowers! I mean. [*xHeucherella alba* 'Bridget Bloom']

"How should I overwinter those pink flowers?"
"What are they?"
" I don't know. You sold them to us."

I love this one. It's a local saying now, as one old farmer couldn't say scentless chamomile; he always said senseless shlamolee.
[It's a local weed and there are government signs on the road to eradicate it whenever possible]

"Do you have Dick Tamus–the one with the gas?" [*Dictamnus*]

"Do y'all have any perenicals?"

"Do ya have any hanging labia?"
 [*Lobelia* –Dan]

"Do you have "Various symptoms" – [I'm not kidding–*Symphytum x uplandicum* 'Variegatum']
"And no, I didn't have any various symptoms; they are hard to come by in this area."

Pride's Corner Nursery had a contest to see who could come up with the most creative planting for their Portapotty garden. A few of the plantings:
Hosta 'Ryan's Big One'
Eupatorium rugosum 'Chocolate'
Rosa 'Golden Showers'
and the ultimate,
Heuchera 'Dale's strain' [icky poo–Dan]

I have two for you, not dirty, though: 1. One of our customers asked for some wake-up robins. (*Trillium erectum*) 2. I once worked in the pond department of a garden center north of Toronto, where we were told by more than one customer that blue herrings were eating their gold fish. I'm guessing this might be what happens to a red herring in the winter?

A few years ago, a little old lady came into our nursery wanting some M&M's™. I sent her down the street to the nearest Seven-Eleven store, but she kept on insisting that it was a flower. After talking with her for a while, she conveyed to me that it was a small bulb, and after further deductions, we found out that it was "anemones" that she wanted. But of course she replied, "Yes, that's what they is, 'M&M's™'."

Last year I had a lady in her twenties (maybe blond), ask for a small Christmas tree. I explained that I no longer carried real small trees but that I could take one of my 7-foot trees and cut it down. As serious as she could be, she looked at me and said, "Won't it look kind of funny with the top flattened out?" As serious as I could be, which was very difficult, I responded by saying "Don't worry, we'll cut it on the bottom."

You know you're a true gardener when instead of going bar-hopping with your friends, you go nursery hopping for a *really* good time! You return home loaded (with plants) and the buzz is from the bees!

From Picadilly Farm ...

"I read that you are known for your roses." (We sell lenten roses or hellebores. They have nothing to do with being a rose.) "They are not roses! Why are they called that?"

"I bought some hellebores from you a year or so ago, planted them on a steep bank, and they now look terrible." (How did you prepare the soil?) "I added soil conditioner." (Tell me exactly what that was.) "Soil conditioner. It looks like dirt." (For our soils, you need to add a lot of organic matter, such as Nature's Helper, rather than mineral soil. I assume they are planted in a shady situation.) "No, they are on a dry bank in full sun."

"The hellebores I got from you were yellow, look terrible, and have not grown!" (Do you have them under an automatic sprinkler? This is a common problem.) "Yes, they're well watered. The sprinkler is set to run 15 minutes each day."

Do you still have any of Mrs. Bradshaw's Gums? I saw them here last time and they looked so pink and healthy. [Geum 'Mrs. J. Bradshaw' A.G.M.]

If We're Not Open, We're Closed (from Picadilly Farm)

"When are you open?" (We are open March through May, Fridays and Saturdays only, 10 to 4.) "Are you open on Sundays?"

"When are you open?" (Again, same answer.) "You are not open on a weekday?" (Friday, I recall, is a weekday.)

It is 4:40 on a retail Saturday. We closed at 4:00, and I am doing the bank deposit, anxious for my gin and tonic, when the phone rings. "We live in Athens and have been trying to get out to Picadilly all day We know you close at 4:00. Are you a *little bit* open?"

"You're not open in the summer! What do you do, go off on vacation and do nothing!"

THE GARDEN CLERK'S DICTIONARY

Y'all got any of them aloha vera Plants?

With apologies to the customers who asked for them, and sympathy for the clerks who had to translate and hold back the tears. The following requests are best preceded by: *"Y'all got any of them . . ."*

acer maples \AY-sir MAY-pulls\ (redundantly redundant)
     maples
achilla jilla \uh-KILL-a-jill-a\ (not a Hun)
     Aquilegia, the columbine
achillian \uh-KILL-ee-un\ (not a Hun, either)
     Achillea, the yarrow
achill-ya \uh-KILL-yuh\
     (make sure they don't have a gun in their hand
     when they say this)
     Achillea, the yarrow
aghastashay \uh-GAWST-uh-shay\
     (usually pronounced with a New England accent)
     Agastache \uh-GAS-ta-key\ the anise hyssop
agravatum \ AH-grav-ay-tum\ (don't get mad!)
     Ageratum, the flossflower
ahsteebles \ Ah-stee-bulls\ (don't wear red around these!)
     Astilbes, the false spirea
aloha vera \ UH-low-ha VER-uh\
     (must cure Hawaiian sunburn as well!)
     Aloe vera, the burn plant
almond joy \ ALL-mund JOY\
     (sometimes you feel like a nut)
     Sedum 'Autumn Joy', stonecrop
alpatiens \ ALL-pay-shuns\
     (I thought this was a type of dog)
     Impatiens, touch-me-not
amnesia \ am-NEE-shuh\ (I forgot about this one)
     Artemesia, wormwood

anals and preanals \ AY-nuls and PREE-a-nuls \
  (I won't EVEN go there!)
  Annuals and perennials
anna moans \ ana- MOANS \ (Does she?)
  Anemones, windflowers
anna mohneys \ ana- moh-NEES \
  (what Ball Seed supplies)
  Anemones, windflowers
anonymous \ uh-NON-ih-muss \ (who wrote this?)
  Euonymus, winter creeper
  Scale food
asher campus tree \ A-sher CAM-pus tree \
  (at least it's well-read)
  Acer campestre, hedge maple
aynohmees \ AY-no-mees \ (I know me)
  Anemone, windflower
arborvishas \ ar-bor-VISH-ahs \
  (. . . jes' one more shot of whishkey)
  Arborvitae, tree of life, aka spider mite food
ascephalus \ ASS-ke-fall-us \ (my ass did this once)
  Asclepias, milkweed
ashleebias \ ASH-leeb-ee-us \
  (found on the Wednesday before Lent?)
  Asclepias, milkweed
astibulls \ AH-stee-bulls \ (are we missing the "spumante"?)
  Astilbes, the false spirea
astilbs \ AH-stilbs \ (somewhat incomplet)
  Astilbes, the false spirea
astrobull \ ASS-tro-bull \ (male space cows)
  Astilbes, the false spirea
astrolobes \ ASS-trow-lobes \ (ears from space?)
  Astilbes, the false spirea
asylum \ uh-SIGH-lum \
  (what you want when you hear these words)
  Alyssum, candytuft

baptismea \ bap-TIS-mee-uh\
    (redneck lupines–Tony Avent)
    Baptisia, the false indigo
barbarian bush \ bar-BARE-ee-yun bush\
    (as seen on Conan)
    Barberry, *Berberis*–aka the bearberry or the ouch plant
beduleeya \ bed-OOL-ee-yuh\   (won't bejewel ya)
    Buddleja, butterfly bush
    British Columbian weed
begohnighya \ be-GOH-nigh-yuh\
    (do de name "Ruby" ring a bell?)
    Begonia, uh, the begonia
berjamoe \ burr-juh-MO\   (le French pronunciation)
    Bergamot or *Monarda*, what puts the yum in Earl Grey Tea

"Binaca Rose"

binaca rose \ bih-NAH-ka rose\
    (handy for those embarrassing breath problems!)
    Rosa 'Bonica', pink everblooming rose

blue jupiter–the rug kind \ BLU- JOOP-ih-ter\
    (interplanetary!)
    Blue rug juniper

bosnia tree \ BOZ-nee-uh tree\   (a true survivor!)
    Bonsai \ BONE-sigh\ tree

brown grass \BROWN grass\   (related to "dead" grass)
    Carex, usually a brown, New Zealand species

caliber \CAL-ih-burr\ adj. (a shot in the dark!)
    Caliper, a way of measuring a tree's trunk width measured
    at a specific height usually (6"-12" above the ground)

campus radicals \CAM-pus RAD-ih-culls\
    (terrorist university vines)
    Campsis radicans, trumpet creeper

candyturf \CAN-dee-turf\
    (Hansel and Gretel–eat your heart out!)
    Iberis, candytuft

caneuhs \CANE-uhs\   (used extensively in Singapore)
    cannas, Indian shot plant

canine peppers \KAY-nine pep-perz\   (For hot dogs!)
    Cayenne peppers

carex buckaninny \KAY-rex BUCK-uh-nin-ee\   (Yee hah!)
    Carex buchananii, A New Zealand sedge

carex hysterical \KAY-rex hih-STARE-ih-cull\
    (. . stop yer cryin')
    Carex hystricina, the porcupine sedge (*Hystrix* means
    porcupine)

carex voluptuous \KAY-rex vole-UP-tyu-us\
    (wolf whistle)
    Carex vulpinoides

carydipteris \KAY-ree-dip-ter-is\   (I'm hip to this!)
    Caryopteris, blue mist shrub

cemetery plant \SEM-uh-tare-ee plant\
    (It hears dead people)
    Thuja plicata, red cedar

"Canine Peppers"

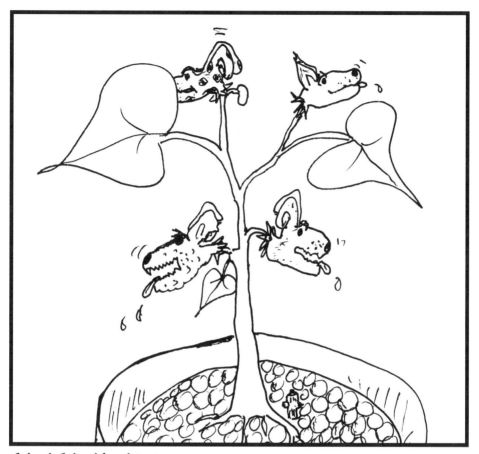

chimichimifugi \chim-ee-chim-ee-FOO-gi\
    (isn't that a type of sushi?)
      Cimicifuga (now *Actaea*)
Chris Farly rose \kris FAR-lee rose\
    (Heavy and humorous buds)
      Rosa 'The Fairy'
clamato \klam-AY-toe\   (you want crackers with that?)
      Clematis
clemantis \kla-MAN-tiss\   (praying?)
      Clematis
cleemitis \klee-MY-tiss\   (some miticide might help?)
      Clematis

clematris \klem-MA-tris\   (can we sleep on it?)
  Clematis

climb a lot \KLIME-uh-lot\   (it does do that)
  Clematis

clitoris \klih-TOR-us\   (back to anatomy for you!)
  Clematis

colorooteeya \kuh-lo-ROOT-ee-yuh\   (which color?)
  Koelreuteria \KUR-luh-roo-tear-ee-yuh\,
  Japanese pagoda tree

corielopsis \ko-REE-lop-sis\   (from Korea?)
  Coreopsis, the tickweed

cotton easter pine on a stick \as it says\
  (does it come with colored eggs?)
  Cotoneaster standard

David eyes \DAY-vid eyes\   (I see)
  Viburnum davidii, David's Viburnum

dead grasses \ded grass-ez\   (why buy them, then?)
  Any of the brown New Zealand sedges

dickandkondra \as it says\ (such a nice couple)
  Dichondra

dickerbocker \DIK-er-bock-er\   (how appropriate)
  Dieffenbachia , the dumbcane

dianthusis \dy-AN-thuss-es\   (is this the plural?)
  Dianthus, carnations, pinks

distilled bees \dis-TILD beez\   (like honey?)
  Astilbe, moisture loving perennial

dodecathalon \doe-deh-CATH-a-lon\ (a new hort sport?)
  Dodecatheon

dog-pecker plant \yeah . . \   (unfortunately accurate)
  Polygonatum odoratum 'Variegatum', solomon's seal

drooping louis \DROOP-ing loo-ee\   (one to pick up!)
  Leucothoe, dog-hobble

ef'in thea \EF-in- thee-yuh\   (f'in nice plant!. .)
  Euphorbia 'Efanthia', a compact form from Proven
  Winners®

eucaleepetus \ yew-KAL-lee-pee-tus \
  (strummed by Hawaiians?)
    Eucalyptus, gum tree

"Eucalipstick"

eucalipstick \ yew-kuh-LIP-stik \
  (What girl Koala bears wear?)
    Eucalyptus, gum tree
evergreen petunias \ um, okay \   (in summer maybe)
    We're still working on this one!
father gilliam \ FAH-thur GILL-ee-yum \
  (grows by the church)
    Fothergilla , the witch alder (which alder?)

fellatio bush \fell-AY-shee-yo bush\ (This name sucks!)
Fallopia japonica, knotweed

fister jupiters \FISS-ter JOOP-e-ters\
(look for the big red spots)
Pfitzer junipers, *Juniperus* 'Pfitzeriana'

flippin' dulas \FLIP-in DYOO-luhs\
(comes with its own spatula! . .)
Filipendulas , meadowsweet

flirs \FLERS\ (grand or noble?)
flowers

florgasm \FLOR-gaz-em\ (Odd noises)
A distinct oo'ing or moaning usually uttered by plant
people admiring a special flower

for Cynthia \for-SIN-thee-yah\
(the one with the yellow flirs)
Forsythia \for-SYTHE-ee-yuh\ (suffer), golden bells

fruit cocktail tree \as it says\
(where's the pineapple?)
Multigraft fruit tree

Fuchsia 'Nylon Rose' \as it says\ (kinda fakey)
Fuchsia 'Neyron Rose'

fuksha \FUHK-sha\ (What the?)
Fuchsia \FOOKS-sha\ (suffer again, it was named after
Fuchs), a.k.a. lady's earrings

funky lilies \FUNK-ee LILL-ees\ (Get down!)
Hosta , plantain lilies, funkias

gerlilies \GUR-lil-eez\ (A perfect match for the boyses)
daylilies?

germaniums \GER-mane-ee-yums\ (rare earth metals)
geraniums

gladiators \GLAD-ee-ay-tors \ (Do well in rings)
Gladioli

gold bushes \as it says\ (makes sense)
Forsythia \for-SYTHE-ee-yuh\, golden bells

74

gonorrhea \GONE-o-ree-ya\ (no clapping!)
  Gomphrena, globe amaranthus
granola maples \gruh-NO-luh mape-elz\ (far out!)
  Acer tataricum ssp. ginnala
hacking grass \as it says\ (cough, cough!)
  Hakonechloa \haw-CO-nay-clo-ah\
  Japanese forest grass

"Hannukahchloa"

hannukahchloa \hah-noo-kah-CLO-ah\ (but is it kosher?)
  Hakonechloa, Japanese forest grass
hawsteses \HAW-stis-is\ (southern entertainers?)
  Hosta , plantain lilies

hebaloreboris \heh-buh-LAH-ree-bore iss\
  (wasn't that a telescope?)
  Helleborus, Christmas rose

hell and a whore \as it says\   (not my idea of fun)
  Helleborus, Christmas rose

helleborees \hell-uh-BORE-eez\   (hmmm...)
  Helleborus, Christmas rose

hemockaliss \he-MOCK-a-liss\
  (English accent this time)
  Hemerocallis

hemorrhoid grape \as it says unfortunately\
  (get the H out)
  Himrod Grape

hedge bushes \as it says\   (aren't they all?)
  Generic term for any appropriate hedging material
  usually *Buxus* or boxwood.

hemeraculous \hem-mer-ACK-you-luss\
  (amazing too!)
  Hemerocallis , daylily

herdulleye \her-dull-EYE\   (just watch her sharp one!)
  Fertilizer

hessias \HESH-uhs\   (watch out, George W!)
  hedging plants

hews   \HEWZ\   (any color will do!)
  Yews , *Taxus*

high geraniums \as it says\
  (this is what happens when you interplant *Cannabis*!)
  Hydrangeas

hinoki grass \huh-NO-kee grass\
  (a *Chamaecyparis* relative?)
  Hakonechloa \haw-CO-nay-clow-ah\,
  Japanese forest grass

hootenanny \HOOT-in-nan-nee\   (sing along!)
  Houttuynia, chameleon plant

76

horthornes \HORE-thorns\
    (they should clean their beds more often!)
    Hawthornes, *Crataegus*
hostis \HOZ-tis\   (yes,they is. . . .)
    Hostas

"Hot biscuits shrub"

hot biscuits shrub \hot-BIS-kits SHRUB\
    (Does it smell good too?)
    Hibiscus, marsh mallow
hummus \HOO-muss\   (great on pita!)
    humus
hydrangellas \HIGH-dran-jel-uhs\   (see hygraniums)
    Hydrangeas

hygraniums \HIGH-gray-ni-yums\
    (see high geraniums)
    Hydrangeas
jallypeenos \jall-ee-PEE-nose\   (goes well in take-ohs)
    Jalapeno peppers
japonicas \juh-PON-ih-cuss\   (. . .)
    Any plant ending in "japonica" (requires detective work)
junifers \JEW-ni-ferz\   (these bloom before Julyifers)
    Junipers
juniors \JEWN-yerz\   (smaller forms)
    Junipers
jupiters \JEW-pi-terz\   (big, round things)
    Junipers
karoosa regale \kuh-ROO-suh ree-gale\
    (wasn't he that singer in the twenties?)
    Hosta 'Krossa Regal'
k-rax \KAY-racks\   (available at K-Mart)
    Carex
lavatory \as it says\
    (didn't we have these in grade school?)
    Lavatera , Rose mallow
lazy-eyed susan \ as it says \
    (git outta yer bed- and bloom!)
    Thunbergia, Black-eyed Susan
liatris pick-yer-nose \lie-AY-tris\
    (I hope it doesn't have green flowers)
    Liatris pycnostachya , Blazing Star
lick yeranea \lik-yer-AY-ne-uh\
    (I also don't want to go there)
    Ligularia , also known as groundsel
limerick ruby \lim-er-ick ROO-bee\
    (There once was a plant from Nantucket)
    Coreopsis 'Limerock Ruby'
liriop \LEER-ee-op\   (...)
    Liriope muscari

litchness \LITCH-ness\ (which ness?)
    Lychnis , Campion
lithium \LITH-ee-yum\
    (I hear it's good for bipolar disorders)
    Lythrum, loosestrife
lungwurst \LUNG-wurst\ (better than Braunschweiger?)
    Pulmonaria, lungwort
lupenis \lew-PEEN-is\
    (Willy, it ain't what you're thinking of!)
    Lupinus

"Martian verbitas"

martian verbitas \MAR-shun ver-BEET-us\
    (the truth from space?)
    Mission arborvitae

mitosis sylvantica \MY-tose-iss sil-VAN-ti-ca\
(time to split!)
Myosotis sylvatica, forget-me-not

mongolias \mon-GOLE-ee-yuhs\
(I guess it IS part of China)
Magnolias

mughoes \MUG-hoes\ (Something pimps do?)
Pinus mugo \mew-go\

mungo pine \mun-GO pine\
(wasn't he in "Blazing Saddles"?)
Pinus mugo, Mugho pine

myassitisa Pinky \my-ASS-it-is-uh PINK-ee\
(who looked?)
Myosotis scorpoides 'Pinky'

"Nagging cherries"

nagging cherries \as it says \ (pitch, pitch, pitch)
Prunus tomentosa , Nanking cherry

nausea \as it says \ (pukey color)
    Knautia, Macedonian scabious

"Nicotina "

nicotina \as it says \ (Smokin'!)
    Nicotiana, flowering tobacco
nike-blue hydrangea \as it says\
    (warning, the colors run on this form)
    Hydrangea macrophylla 'Nikko Blue' -just a faster grower
nymphophia \as it says \
    (keep this away from the 'pokers')
    Kniphofia \knip-HOF-ee-ya\ red-hot poker

packastranda \pak-a-STRAN-duh \ (I think I packed one)
Pachysandra

panties \as it says \ (unmentionable)
Peonies?

patty's bum poppy \as it says\ (usually bent over)
Patty's Plum Poppy

penis \PEEN-is\ (our local form is P. contorta!)
Pinus (European pronunciation)

penisetums \PEE-nis-eat-ums\ (Do they?)
Pennisetum, an ornamental grass

penisites \PEE-nis-eye-tees\
(people who say this don't know dick)
Pennisetum, an ornamental grass

penstemom \PEN-sti-mom\ (get one for penstedad!)
Penstemon

perestroika plant \as it says\ (used in Russia?)
Perovskia, Russian Sage

persecuted himalayan fleeced flowers \as it says\
(Archie Bunker is among us)
Persicaria affinis (Himalayan Fleece-flower)

petuniaster \as it says\ (Some hybrid!)
Petunia

pickle weeds \as it says\ (could be dill?)
Pontaderia, the pickerel weed

pineys \PAH-nees\ (for the fjords?)
Peonies, southern dialect

pissyback \as it says\ (grows by colored snow?)
Tolmiea menziesii, the piggyback plant

platycondom \plat-ee-CON-dom\ (from Troy?)
Platycodon , hilariously, the "balloon" flower

"Pompous ass grass "

pompous ass grass \as it says\ (hmpf!)
    Cortaderia selloana or pampas grass
poormeum \POUR-me-um\ (penniless, sigh)
    Phormium, New Zealand Flax
popular \as it says\ (and admired)
    Poplar tree
potentia \po-TEN-ti-yuh\ (strong Hispanic aunt)
    Potentilla, cinquefoil
potentillo \po-TEN-ti-loh\ (strong form of armadillo)
    Potentilla, cinquefoil

pre-annuals \as it says\
    (do these come up before the others?)
    Perennials you know, they come back every year
privy bush \as it says\   (perfect next to the outhouse)
    Ligustrum vulgare or the privet
prostate spruce \as it says\
    (I would think that would hurt)
    Picea glauca 'Pendula' or prostrate blue spruce
pullonmalaria \pul-ON-muh-LAIR-ee-yuh\ (no way!)
    Pulmonaria
purple uterus plant \as it says\
    (now Terra Nova has new colors!)
    Purple heuchera
rapist palm \as it says\   (best kept in jailhouses)
    Rhapis excelsa, a palm
red bird bushes \as it says\   (go cardinals!)
    Cercis, redbud
rhododingdong \RO-DO-ding-dong\
    (the witch is dead)
    Rhododendron
rhody catawobblis \RO-dee CAT-uh-WOB-bil-is\
    (so, stay off the catnip!)
    Rhododendron catawbiense
rondo grass mat \as it says\   (sounds like a TV offer)
    Ophiopogon or mondo grass
rosydendrums \ROE-see-DEN-drums\
    (you need colored glasses to see them)
    Rhododendrons
rubadeka \RUB-uh-dek-uh\   (better than the plastic deka)
    Rudbeckia, the black-eyed Susan
rubadekia \RUB-uh-dek-ee-uh\   (you're so fine)
    Rudbeckia, the black-eyed Susan
rushing sage \as it says\   (used by football teams)
    Perovskia, the Russian sage

saliva \as it says\   (this pronunciation makes me spit!)
Salvia splendens, usually

samaragdags arbervitee \SAM-ar-ag-dags AHR-ber-veet-ee\
(yah, goes well with lutefisk!)
Thuja occidentalis 'Smargd' arborvitae

scabieola \SKAY-bee-oh-luh\
(don't let it near your skin!)
Scaveola

screw yous \as it says\
(watch your use of such plants in mixed company!)
Spiral topiary Taxus (yews)

scuffy dimes \as it says\   (shiny ones are better)
Scuppernong grapes

"Sega palm"

sega palm \as it says\   (Popular with teenagers)
Commonly, *Cycas revoluta* or sago palm

slab o' flahrs \SLAY-ub uh flahrs\
  (another southern specialty)
  Flat of annuals

sleebum \as it says\ (a nasty-ass weed)
  Silybum marianum or milk thistle

sloppy galoshes \as it says\
  (neat ones are much nicer)
  Salpiglossis

snackdragons \as it says\
  (do these give you heartburn?)
  Antirrhinum or snapdragons

snowblob tree \as it says\
  (do three make a snow man?)
  Styrax japonica

sod patties \as it says\ (for your vegetarian friends)
  Sod squares, yum!

soxifraggleitch \SOCKS-uh-frag-gull-itch\ (Yiddish?)
  Saxifrage

spagnum \SPAG-num\ (Short for tasty spaghetti?)
  Sphagnum moss

stella-de-oreo \as it says\ (black and white Stella?)
  Hemerocallis 'Stella de Oro' (Daylily)

stewartia studio-camellia \as it says\
  (must be on Martha's TV show)
  Stewartia pseudocamellia

stripped yer carcass \as it says\
  (for Hannibal Lector? Ewww)
  Streptocarpus (a great houseplant)

sylvia argentina \as it says\ (Don't cry for me)
  Salvia argentea

sylvia cocksineh \SILL-vee-yuh COCKS-in-eh\
  (nasty and a bit Canadian)
  Salvia coccinea

tee-ollies \as it says\ (Goes well with tea "Laurels")
  Tea olives

"Stella-de-oreo"

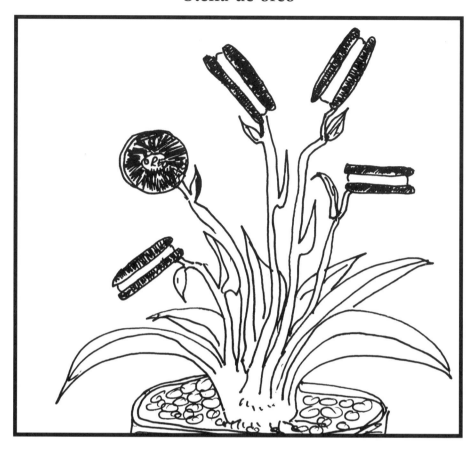

tellim imaglandifloora \as it says\ (no, YOU tell him!)
    Tellima grandiflora
that hemorrhoid plant \as it says\
    (fertilize daily with Preparation H®)
    Hemerocallis or daylily
that white thing \as it says\
    (you know, the one with the flowers?)
    Bacopa, or any other white blooming plant
theresa bug-net rose \as it says\
    (catches butterflies?)
    Rosa 'Thérèse Bugnet' \boo-NYAY\

tumps \as it says\
    (overalls required to pronounce this word)
    Turnips

urea bush \you-REE-uh bush\   (never need fertilizing!)
    Taxus or yew

verbatims \as it says\   (tell the truth, the whole truth)
    Viburnum

verbumasskum \ver-BUM-ass-kum\ (icky)
    Verbascum

vibratum careless spies \as it says\
    (Found hiding under garden beds)
    Viburnum carlesii, the Korean spice viburnum

vina-sinus \VINE-uh SINE-us\
    (fertilize this with Sudafed ®)
    Vinca minor

wannamus \WAN-uh-muss\   (s—ure, why not?)
    Euonymus

wax-eared privates \as it says\
    (hopefully the army will clean these up)
    Ligustrum or wax-leaf privet

white creeping hairballs \as it says\
    (also found under beds)
    Campanula carpatica, the white Carpathian harebells

whore's drawers \as it says\
    (goes up and down throughout the growing season)
    Viburnum opulus or *V. tomentosum*

whorry rocks \HORE-ee ROKS\
    (mind yer wallet when climbing these)
    Hollyhocks

wigglea or wigla or wiggilya \as it says\
    (wasn't there a game called Uncle Wiggilya?)
    Weigela \why-GEEL-uh\

your onamus \YER ON-uh-muss\
    (at least it isn't MY onamus)
    Euonymus

zaylyers \ZAYL-yers\ (not to be confused with sailors)
Azaleas

"White creeping hairballs"

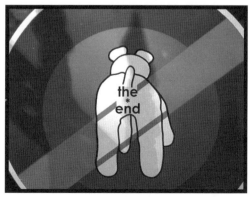